The Greenville Giant

James Noble ■ Jonatronix

OXFORD
UNIVERSITY PRESS

Max, Cat, Ant and Tiger were captured by Dr X's X-craft.

They managed to defeat the on-board X-bots and steer the ship away from NASTI – but Dr X re-programmed the X-craft to autopilot.

The X-craft brought them into NASTI and Dr X forced them to give up their watches.

Dr X used their watches to power his X-machine. He shrunk their school before moving on to his next target – the whole world!

Dani Day rescued the children from their cell and they disabled the X-machine and accidentally shrunk Dr X to micro-size!

Dr X was handed over to the police and was sent to prison.

Chapter 1 – A visitor

Dr X sat in the visiting room at Greenville Prison. He was feeling very glum. His mother, Mrs X, was at the door, smiling sweetly at the guard.

"It's just a lemon sponge cake," she said, as she held up the cake. "You wouldn't stop a mother giving her dearest son his favourite cake, would you?"

Dr X groaned and put his head in his hands. Even super-villains could have embarrassing mums!

Mrs X approached the table. "Hello, my darling boy," she cooed. Dr X cringed some more as he felt the eyes of the prison's other super-villains on him. "I've brought you your favourite treat."

As his mum set the cake down on the table, Dr X leaned forward eagerly – but not because he wanted to eat the cake.

No, the cake was going to come in useful for something else …

Chapter 2 – A mysterious note

Later that day, at NICE HQ …

Dani Day turned to Inspector Textor. "I don't get it," she said.

"Watch again carefully," said the inspector. He replayed the footage on the monitor.

Dani saw Dr X sitting in the visiting room at Greenville Prison. His mother put a cake on the table. Dr X reached for it so eagerly, he knocked it on to the floor. It landed with a *splat* and the cake went everywhere.

"Look," said Textor, as he pressed pause. "The guard steps forward to clean up the mess. He doesn't see Dr X slip his arm under the table."

The inspector tapped at his keyboard and zoomed in on the piece of paper that Mrs X had taken from her son. "He gave her a message," he said.

Dani peered at the screen and saw …

Dani frowned. "What should we do?"

"I want to search NASTI," said the inspector. "There must be a reason that he gave his mother that map – maybe he wants her to find something."

"NASTI has been securely locked up since Dr X was put in prison," Dani pointed out. "There's no way his mother could get inside …" She paused. "Or is there?"

"I wouldn't be surprised if Dr X has a secret entrance," Inspector Textor replied.

Dani agreed it was better to be safe than sorry. "Let's check it out, then."

They went down to the basement of NICE and entered Dr X's old lair.

"Everything looks the same," said the inspector, as they wandered around NASTI.

"I'm getting a bad feeling," said Dani, "but I can't quite put my finger on it."

Behind them, Mrs X lurked in a dark corner. She was pressed flat against a wall. Her nervous breathing grew louder and louder. Yet neither Inspector Textor nor Dani noticed the intruder hidden in the shadows.

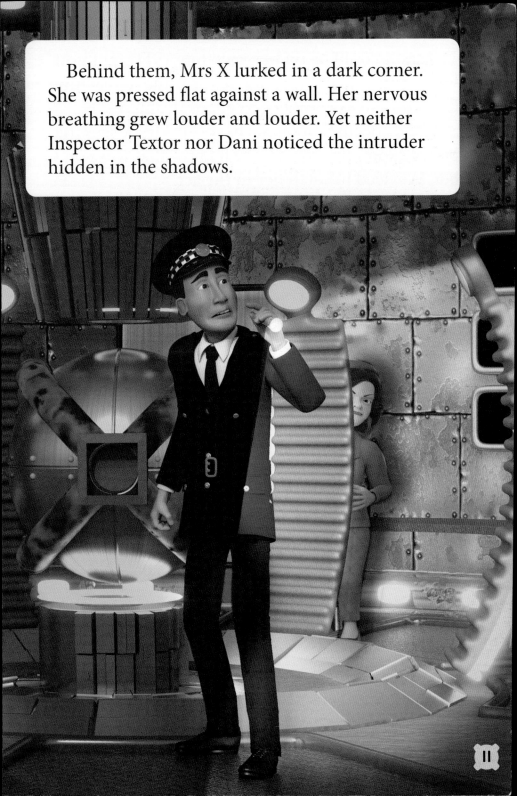

"Mrs X could be on her way to NASTI right now," said Dani. "We can't let her get near the X-machine. Can you call extra police to guard the place?"

The inspector shook his head. "If Mrs X sees the police snooping around, she'll know that we're on to her. We need to catch her in the act."

Dani grinned as they walked out of NASTI.

"I know just who can help."

Chapter 3 – A new mission

PING! Max, Cat, Ant and Tiger huddled around the computer.

"It's an email from Dani," Max said.

Since Dr X had been locked up, they hadn't heard much from Dani. In fact, their lives had been rather quiet – almost boring.

"It would be fun to have a new adventure," Tiger said, grinning.

"It sounds quite serious," Cat murmured. "Dani's never asked us to be quite so secretive before."

Hi guys!
We need your help urgently at NICE HQ – it's very important that you are not seen by anybody.
Your friend,
Dani Day

"Let's go in the micro-buggy," Max suggested. "It's been a while since we took it for a spin."

The friends turned the dials on their watches. They pushed the X and ...

Soon after …

The micro-friends zoomed through the streets of Greenville. They veered around shopping bags and people's stomping feet. Max had to swerve violently to avoid the big, slobbery mouth of a dog who clearly fancied them for lunch.

Cat laughed at how pale Tiger had gone. "Don't worry," she said. "We got past it."

"It would have been pretty big, even if we weren't micro-size!" grumbled Tiger.

The friends parked the micro-buggy down a well-hidden alley close to NICE. They spotted a tiny Dani waving at them from behind a discarded can.

"Why are you micro-sized?" Max asked, as they all hid behind the can. It wasn't often that Dani shrank, too.

"Shhh," whispered Dani, ushering them into the shadows. "I'm on surveillance. We think Mrs X might try to break into NASTI using a map Dr X gave her."

"A map of NASTI?" asked Ant.

Dani nodded. "Look at this copy of the map. The X-machine is circled and there is another strange symbol on it but we're not sure what it means. I need to figure out what Dr X is planning whilst you guys …"

"Keep watch?" Max asked.

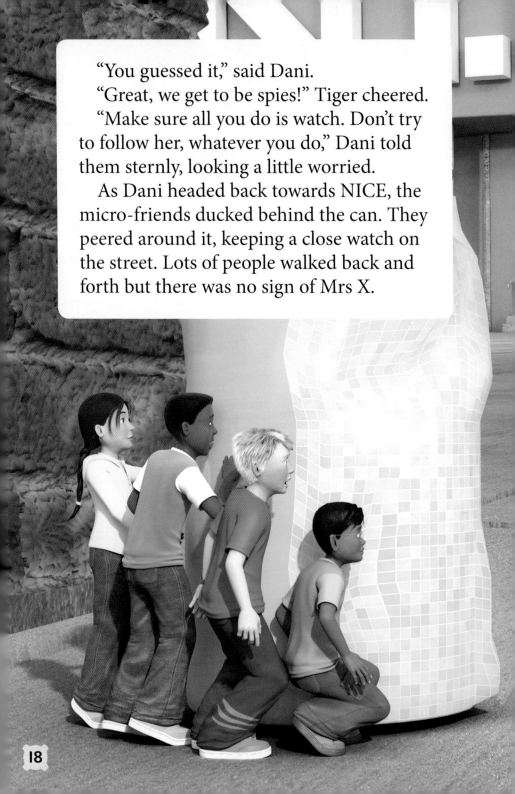

"You guessed it," said Dani.

"Great, we get to be spies!" Tiger cheered.

"Make sure all you do is watch. Don't try to follow her, whatever you do," Dani told them sternly, looking a little worried.

As Dani headed back towards NICE, the micro-friends ducked behind the can. They peered around it, keeping a close watch on the street. Lots of people walked back and forth but there was no sign of Mrs X.

Tiger sighed. "Being a spy isn't as exciting as I'd imagined. We've been here for hours and nothing's happened!"

"It's only been 15 minutes," Ant laughed, nudging his friend.

"Quiet!" Cat glared at them. "Look over there!"

Dr X's bumbling henchmen, Plug and Socket, were heading towards NICE. They looked nervous and their eyes darted around to make sure they weren't being followed.

"They're definitely up to something," said Max, as the friends carefully followed the henchmen right up to the building.

Max, Cat, Ant and Tiger gasped when they saw the two men walk up to the wall and disappear through it.

"That's impossible," whispered Cat.

The children raced forward. In the wall, an X-shaped door made of bricks was slowly closing.

"Of course!" said Max. "That's what that X meant – the map showed another entrance to NASTI."

"We need to follow them!" Tiger yelled.

"We should tell Dani …" Ant started.

"There's no time," Max told them. "Come on!"

The friends raced through the secret door just before it snapped firmly shut.

Chapter 4 – In the dark

"Where are the lights?" Plug groaned, as the henchmen stumbled along a dark corridor.

Socket reached out blindly to check the walls – and accidentally hit Plug in the face.

"Watch it!" said Plug.

"I'm looking for the light switch," Socket responded.

"Well it's not on my face," Plug grumbled.

"YOU TWO LAZY SO-AND-SOS!" a voice boomed.

Plug and Socket jumped, startled. Up ahead, they could just make out the shadowy shape of Mrs X.

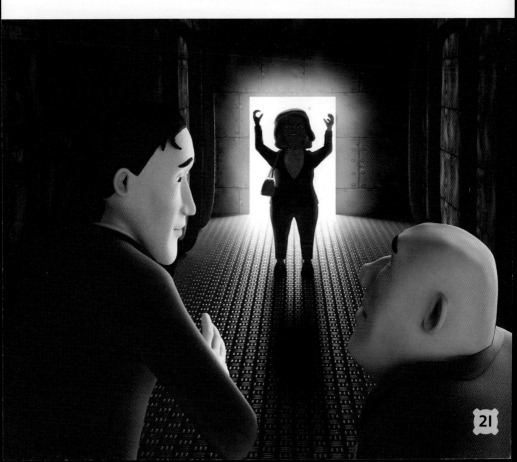

"I've been waiting for this moment for a long time," growled Mrs X. "My poor darling son is in prison and all because of you two blundering oafs."

Plug and Socket looked guilty. "But it wasn't our …"

"Silence!" ordered Mrs X. "It's lucky for you I'm such a forgiving person." She stepped forward, grinning evilly. "You can make it up to my son but only if you do exactly what I say. For now, I want you to hide and wait for my signal …"

Plug and Socket looked at each other. They had a feeling Mrs X was going to be even worse to work for than Dr X.

Meanwhile …

The micro-friends sneaked along the dark corridor. Being inside NASTI again was making them uneasy. This is where they had been on some of their most dangerous and frightening adventures.

There was no time to worry, though. They needed to stop Mrs X, even if they didn't yet know what she was planning to do. They reached the entrance to Dr X's lair and crept silently inside.

Dr X's lair looked as eerie as ever. The floating X-machine was still in the centre of the room but it no longer glowed green. They watched as Mrs X plonked herself down in her brand new chair – she'd clearly been making at herself at home. In her hand she cradled a familiar, golden box. The micro-friends knew that there were five slots in the box – one for each of their watches and one for Dani's. If Mrs X was able to steal them, she would have complete control of the X-machine!

"I don't like the look of this," Max whispered.

"I'm so glad you could join us," Mrs X said suddenly. She looked right at the children, smiling nastily. The micro-friends tried to run but Mrs X popped open the gold box. She pushed a button and bright green beams rippled through the room. They passed over the friends' watches, making them crackle dangerously.

Before the friends knew it, a familiar sensation coursed through them and they started to grow.

"Oh no!" they cried.

Chapter 5 – The plan revealed

"There," said Mrs X. "You're much easier to see now." Then she laughed. "My darling son's plan is working perfectly! I raised a real genius."

"A real genius who's locked up in prison," Tiger muttered.

"Not for long," Mrs X cackled, reaching into her pocket and taking out a crumpled piece of paper which she threw towards the children.

Max caught it. "We already know that Dr X gave you a map marking the secret entrance to NASTI," he said.

Mrs X smirked. "Turn it over."

Max looked at the back of the paper and the friends read the scribbled message:

All you have to do is lure the children to NASTI!

"It was a trick," Ant groaned.

All you have to
do is lure the
children to
NASTI!

Max looked nervously towards the X-machine. "You want to restart the X-machine, don't you?"

"You'll never take our watches off us!" Tiger added.

"Don't worry," said Ant, backing right up against the door. "She needs Dani's watch, too."

Mrs X threw back her head, giving her most wicked villainous laugh. "That's what *you* think!"

Mrs X thrust the gold box into the heart of the X-machine. It snapped into place with a chilling clank.

The box started to glow. Then it hummed. Four jagged beams of green light shot across the room like lightning bolts, striking each of the friends' watches.

"Oh no!" gasped Cat, as their watches flickered.

"It's draining the power," Max cried, as he saw the gold light of the box growing brighter and brighter.

Then the X-machine's giant X started to pulse with a sickly green light. Mrs X cackled in triumph. "I've done it!" she cried. "My little Cuthbert is going to be ever so proud of his mummy!"

Suddenly, the gold box started jerking and rattling. The X-machine fizzed and smoke filled the air.

"No!" Mrs X gasped. "It's not supposed to do this. It's supposed to …"

She didn't have time to finish because the X-machine started shutting down. Mrs X kicked it. "You stupid machine! Arrrggghhh!"

Mrs X was knocked to the ground as the X-machine fired one last bolt of green light, right at her.

Then everything fell silent.

Chapter 6 – Mrs X, the giant

As the smoke cleared, the friends turned to each other. "Is everyone all right?" Cat asked.

"I think so," said Max.

Ant looked down at his watch. "It looks like our watches are still working," he said.

"Erm, guys," said Tiger, nervously. He pointed at Mrs X who was lying on the floor, groaning in pain. "Shouldn't Mrs X have been shrunk?"

Not only was Dr X's mum not micro-size but she looked like she was actually *growing* …

Plug and Socket ran into the room.

"Was that the signal?" Plug asked.

The henchmen took one look at Mrs X's growing frame and backed away in terror. She seemed to have grown a whole metre in just a few seconds.

"What's happening?" she mumbled, confused.

"You're becoming a … a giant," Socket told her, backing away until he bumped into the wall. He was worried that her temper would grow, along with everything else!

Mrs X smiled. "Well, it looks like I don't need a clever plan to get my son out of prison. I can just use my giant strength."

With that, she lumbered towards the door but she hit her head on the frame. She was too tall for it now. She tried to duck through but her shoulders got stuck – she was too wide for it as well.

Frustrated, she punched at the walls to make enough room for herself. Then she stomped through the Mrs-X-shaped hole in the wall.

"Come with me," she ordered Plug and Socket, who scurried after her, lost in her giant shadow.

Chapter 7 – Tracking the giant

The friends raced outside. They could see Mrs X in the distance, heading straight to Greenville Prison. She was definitely getting bigger!

"We don't have much time," said Max. "It won't take a giant Mrs X long to cover that distance."

"Then she'll be able to break down any wall she wants," Cat fumed. "We have to stop her!"

"But how? She's ginormous!" Tiger said.

"We could use our watches to grow," Max suggested. "Then we might be big enough to stop her."

Ant shook his head. "It's too risky – the technology hasn't been tested. We might never be able to get back to normal size."

The friends looked at each other, wide-eyed. Tiger gulped. "I like being micro-sized but I'm not sure I'd enjoy being *macro*-sized!"

"I've got an idea," said Cat, as she turned and ran back towards NICE.

"What are you doing?" Max shouted after her.

"Take the micro-buggy," she said. "I'm going to fetch the micro-copter. I have a feeling it might come in handy."

Max, Ant and Tiger could hear the cries from far away. It sounded like Mrs X hadn't gone unnoticed.

Max revved the micro-buggy's engine and they zoomed off in search of the giant.

It wasn't long before they found the trail of destruction Mrs X had left behind. Cars had been toppled over like toys and people were running away from her in all directions. Max weaved the micro-buggy in and out of the chaos. The closer they got to the prison, the worse it seemed to become.

"There she is!" shouted Tiger. "She's as tall as a tower block now!"

"There's Greenville Prison." Ant shuddered as the imposing building came into view.

"She's heading right for it," said Max, guiding the micro-buggy towards her.

Mrs X yelped and jumped, almost tripping over as the buggy zipped this way and that. Tiger and Ant had to hold on tight as Max turned the buggy in tight circles driving in and out of Mrs X's huge feet.

"Ow!" Mrs X roared. "You pesky kids!" She stomped her massive foot in anger. It sent a tremor through the ground that made the micro-buggy veer off-course and crash through a bush.

"Ooof!" said Max as he pulled the buggy clear. "Is everyone OK?"

Ant adjusted his glasses. "I'm fine," he said.

"Me too," said Tiger. "Now let's … waaaaahhh!"

Mrs X had reached her giant hand down and scooped up Tiger, dropping him into her giant-sized pocket.

Chapter 8 – The giant's pocket

Inside his prison cell, Dr X could hear yelling and screaming coming from outside. He went to his window.

"Arrrggghhh!" he yelped, backing away.

Mrs X spotted him at his window. "Don't worry, munchkin. Mummy's here. I'll save you!" she called, tenderly.

Dr X scrambled back into his prison bed, pulling the covers over his head. He wasn't sure he wanted to be rescued any more.

Inside Mrs X's pocket, Tiger tumbled over and over. The smell of mints was overpowering. He had to get out. He grabbed two handfuls of fabric and started climbing up the pocket. It was hard work!

He heard Mrs X grumbling. "Stupid fly! Go away!"

"That's no fly," Tiger smiled to himself, recognizing the low hum of the micro-copter. Cat had made it!

Tiger climbed as fast as he could to the top of the pocket. He peered up and saw the micro-copter buzzing around Mrs X's head. Cat swooped down towards him, dropping a paper-clip ladder just above his head. Tiger grabbed on tight as Cat flew up, up, up, dragging him to safety.

Mrs X tried to snatch them from the air but her giant hands were just too slow.

Cat landed the micro-copter safely as Max drew the micro-buggy up alongside. Mrs X was stomping back towards the prison. She was now almost twice the building's height.

Inside the prison, Dr X hid even deeper beneath the covers.

BOOOM!

Mrs X slammed a giant hand on to the roof of the prison, leaving a gaping hole. She reached in and plucked her son from his bed.

Outside the prison, Max, Cat, Ant and Tiger looked at each other anxiously.

"Look," said Ant, pointing down the street. "There's Dani!"

A familiar figure came racing towards them, holding the gold box in both hands. "Mrs X left this behind," Dani wheezed, struggling to catch her breath. "I think we can use it to create enough power to shrink her."

The friends quickly placed their watches into the slots and stood back.

"Ready?" Dani asked.

The friends were all thinking the same thing: *What if their watches were damaged? This could be the last micro-adventure they ever had …*

"Ready," they said.

Dani leaned down and pressed the button. As the gold box began to fizz and crackle, a huge beam of light shot out and struck Mrs X.

"Noooooooooo!" roared Mrs X as she started to shrink.

Dr X bolted towards the prison guards.
"Take me back to my cell," he shouted.
"*Please!*"

As the guards guided him away, back-up arrived. Mrs X, now back to normal, made a run for it.

"Stop her!" Inspector Textor yelled, as Mrs X darted off towards a black limousine. Two familiar getaway drivers were waiting for her. Mrs X looked back briefly at her son before leaping into the car.

As she sped away, the friends couldn't help but wonder what Mrs X would get up to next.

GREENVILLE NEWS

The Greenville Giant?

Police were baffled after receiving numerous reports that a giant was seen rampaging through Greenville yesterday afternoon. More than a dozen people claim to have seen the larger-than-life figure stomping through the town towards Greenville Prison. It is believed that she was trying to help a prisoner escape.

Greenville's Inspector Textor has assured us that every prisoner remains safely locked away. When asked for a comment, Inspector Textor said: "We are aware of the reports and have been looking into the matter. We can confidently say that the public has no reason to worry."

It has been suggested the clean-up may take some time but NICE have volunteered to lead this.

The clean-up begins.